THE
DECLARATION OF
INDEPENDENCE

by Lori Mortensen ~ illustrated by Matthew Skeens

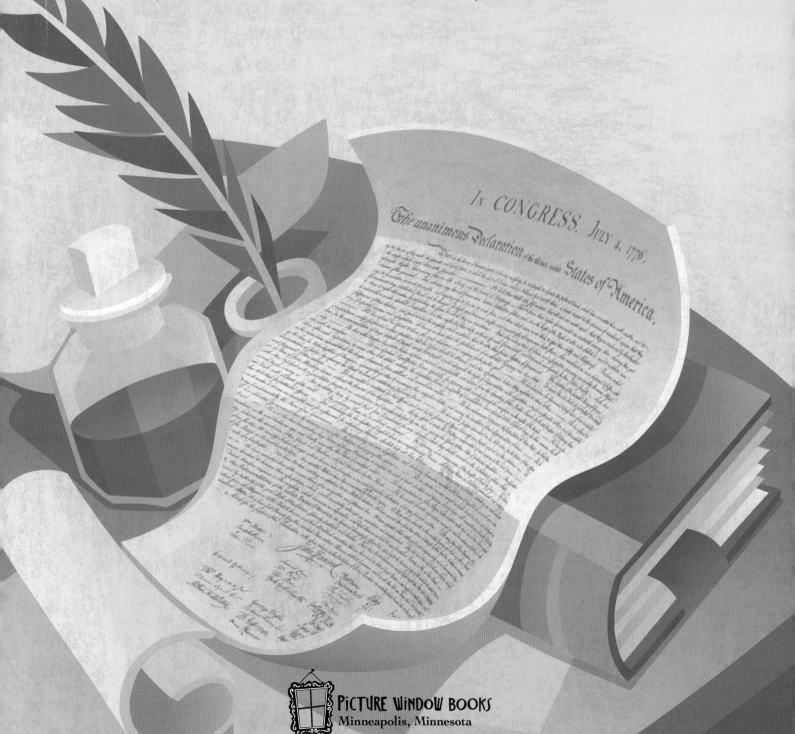

PICTURE WINDOW BOOKS
Minneapolis, Minnesota

Special thanks to our advisers for their expertise:

Kevin Byrne, Ph.D., Professor of History
Gustavus Adolphus College, St. Peter, Minnesota

Terry Flaherty, Ph.D., Professor of English
Minnesota State University, Mankato

Editor: Shelly Lyons
Designer: Nathan Gassman
Page Production: Melissa Kes
Editorial Director: Nick Healy
The illustrations in this book were created digitally.

Picture Window Books
151 Good Counsel Drive
P.O. Box 669
Mankato, MN 56002-0669
877-845-8392
www.picturewindowbooks.com

Printed in the United States of America.

All books published by Picture Window Books
are manufactured with paper containing at least
10 percent post-consumer waste.

Library of Congress Cataloging-in-Publication Data
Mortensen, Lori, 1955-
The Declaration of Independence / by Lori Mortensen ;
   illustrated by Matthew Skeens.
p. cm. — (American Symbols)
Includes bibliographical references and index.
ISBN 978-1-4048-5165-8 (library binding)
1. United States. Declaration of Independence—Juvenile literature.
2. United States—Politics and government—1775-1783—Juvenile literature.
 I. Skeens, Matthew, ill. II. Title.
E221.M68 2009
973.3'13—dc22   2008037906

Table of Contents

My name is Thomas Jefferson. I wrote the Declaration of Independence. Later, I was the third president of the United States. To me, the Declaration of Independence was more important than being president. Its bold words helped the United States of America become a free nation. Listen to this exciting story.

4

What Is the Declaration of Independence?

The Declaration of Independence was written during the Revolutionary War (1775–1783). During this war, Americans fought to break free from Great Britain. The document explains Americans' rights. It says government officials should protect those rights. It also says the United States of America is a free nation.

The Declaration of Independence is one of three documents called the Charters of Freedom. The other two documents included are the U.S. Constitution and the Bill of Rights.

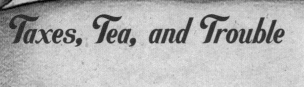

Taxes, Tea, and Trouble

A group of people from Great Britain arrived in North America in the 1600s. They chose to settle there. By about 1770, 2.5 million people lived in 13 colonies along the East Coast. Great Britain's king ruled them.

Many colonists believed the king's laws were unfair. When the king ordered a change in the tax on tea, the colonists fought back. In December 1773, a large group of colonists dressed as Native Americans dumped 342 crates of British tea into Boston Harbor. This event was later called the "Boston Tea Party."

Many colonists disagreed with British laws. The laws said they could buy and sell many goods only from Great Britain.

Fight for Freedom

The colonists' actions angered the king. So the king ordered even tougher laws.

On September 5, 1774, a group of colonists met to talk about the problems between Great Britain and the Colonies. This meeting was called the First Continental Congress. The men wanted peace with Great Britain. However, peace would not come for many years.

Not all colonists wanted to fight against Great Britain. Many thought they should remain loyal to the king.

On April 19, 1775, British soldiers arrived in Lexington, Massachusetts. Colonial soldiers were waiting for them. A shot was fired. The Revolutionary War had begun.

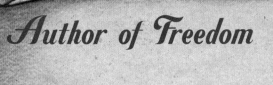

Author of Freedom

Nearly a year later, on June 11, 1776, the Second Continental Congress met in Philadelphia, Pennsylvania. The men decided it was time to break away from Great Britain. They wanted to form a new nation. They asked five men to create an important document. The group chose Thomas Jefferson to write it.

The document would later be called the Declaration of Independence. Once finished, it would help the colonists gain their freedom from Great Britain.

Thomas Jefferson was 33 years old when he wrote the Declaration of Independence. He was one of the youngest members of the Second Continental Congress.

The Finished Document

Jefferson worked on the document for less than 17 days. Then he showed it to the Continental Congress. They argued and made many changes to it. On July 4, 1776, the Continental Congress approved the Declaration of Independence.

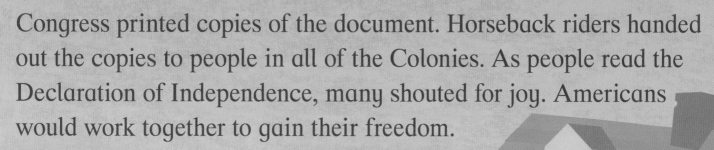

Congress printed copies of the document. Horseback riders handed out the copies to people in all of the Colonies. As people read the Declaration of Independence, many shouted for joy. Americans would work together to gain their freedom.

John Hancock was the first signer of the Declaration of Independence. Some people believe he wrote his name in large letters so the king could read it without his glasses.

The Message

The beginning of the Declaration of Independence describes why it was written. It says that when people must go against their government, they should explain why.

Next, the document states some of the most powerful ideas about human rights ever written. It states that all people are created equal, and everyone has natural rights. Those rights include "Life, Liberty, and the pursuit of Happiness." The document explains how people form governments to protect those rights. Sometimes the government fails to protect the people's rights. Then the people have the right to change the government.

Free and Independent

The document also blames Great Britain's king for failing to protect the colonists' rights. It lists examples of how the king had treated the colonists unfairly.

At the end, the document declares the Colonies "Free and Independent States." It says they have all of the powers of a free nation.

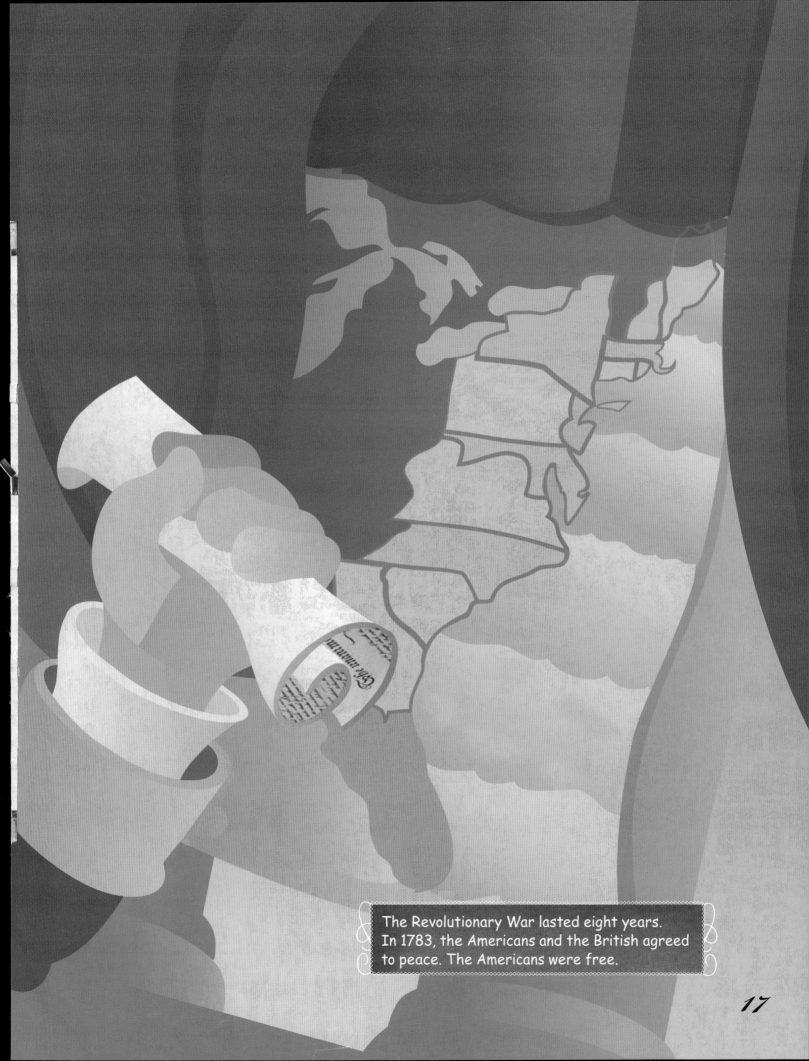

The Revolutionary War lasted eight years. In 1783, the Americans and the British agreed to peace. The Americans were free.

Model for a Nation

Throughout the years, people have looked at the Declaration of Independence as a model. Its words have helped others in their own fight for rights.

In 1848, Elizabeth Cady Stanton fought for women's rights. She used the Declaration of Independence as a guide to write her own document. It states that women have the same rights as men.

During the Civil War (1861–1865), President Abraham Lincoln gave his "Gettysburg Address." In this famous speech, he told Americans to remember the words of the Declaration of Independence.

In 1963, Martin Luther King Jr. fought for black people's rights. He spoke of the Declaration of Independence. "I have a dream … ," he said, " … that all men are created equal."

19

Seeing the Declaration of Independence

Today, visitors can see the Declaration of Independence. It is kept in the National Archives Building in Washington, D.C. The famous document is displayed in a large case along with the U.S. Constitution and the Bill of Rights.

The Declaration of Independence is kept in a huge bulletproof case. At night, it is lowered 22 feet (6.7 meters) into a vault and locked inside.

Americans celebrate their country's birthday on July 4. That is the day Congress approved the Declaration of Independence more than 200 years ago. Today, the Declaration of Independence is a symbol of Americans' struggle for freedom.

Now you know this important story!

Declaration of Independence Facts

The Declaration of Independence was written on parchment made from animal skin. After more than 200 years, the ink has faded and the parchment has cracked. Today, special glass protects it from light. Because air can harm the document, a gas called helium fills the case.

The Declaration of Independence has been moved many times to keep it safe. During World War II (1939–1945), it was kept at Fort Knox, Kentucky, where the nation's reserve gold supply is kept.

Fifty-six men signed the Declaration of Independence. Signing the document was a brave and daring thing to do. It was proof that the men were against the king. If caught, they could have been killed. Twelve of their homes were burned. Many of them lost everything they owned. Nine signers died during the Revolutionary War.

Glossary

Colonies — the 13 groups of people living in North America before the Revolutionary War; they were ruled by Great Britain

colonists — a group of people who settle in another country and remain part of the mother country

Continental Congress — a group of 56 delegates who made important decisions for the 13 colonies and, later, the United States

document — a paper containing important information

independence — free from the control of another

Revolutionary War — (1775–1783) the 13 colonies' fight for independence from Great Britain to become the United States of America

rights — just, moral, or lawful claims

symbol — an object that stands for something else

tax — a fee charged by government

Index

To Learn More

More Books to Read

Klingel, Cynthia Fitterer, and Robert B. Noyed. *The Declaration of Independence.* Chanhassen, Minn.: Child's World, 2002.

Leavitt, Amie Jane. *The Declaration of Independence in Translation: What it Really Means.* Mankato, Minn.: Capstone Press, 2009.

St. George, Judith. *The Journey of the One and Only Declaration of Independence.* New York: Philomel Books, 2005.

On the Web

FactHound offers a safe, fun way to find educator-approved Internet sites related to this book. Here's what you do:

1. Visit *www.facthound.com*
2. Choose your grade level.
3. Begin your search.

This book's ID number is 9781404851658

Look for other books in the American Symbols series:

Angel Island

The Bald Eagle

The Bill of Rights

Ellis Island

The Great Seal of the United States

The Liberty Bell

The Lincoln Memorial

Mount Rushmore

Our American Flag

Our National Anthem

Our U.S. Capitol

The Pledge of Allegiance

The Statue of Liberty

Uncle Sam

The U.S. Constitution

The U.S. Supreme Court

The White House

24

Author and Illustrator

Lori Mortensen is a published author with more than a dozen books to her credit. Lori lives in Northern California with her family and enjoys going on long walks and playing "Around the World" with her three teenagers. To learn more about Lori and her books, visit her Web site: *www.lorimortensen.com*

Matthew Skeens graduated from the Minneapolis College of Art and Design with a BFA in illustration. When he's not drawing, Matthew likes to run, solve mysteries, chase bears, and pogo stick up stairs (but not down). He lives in Des Moines, Iowa, with his wife, Heather, and their orange cat named Calvin.